Núria & Empar Jiménez
Rosa M. Curto

Taking care of your planet

Blow! air

BARRON'S

You dive beneath the water.
One stroke, two strokes, three strokes,
and . . . aaagh! You have to come up for
air. It's a shame you're not a fish, isn't it?
Then you would be able to stay under the
water. You breathe in strongly and feel
the air entering your nose and reaching
your lungs. It's very pleasant to feel
them filling up!

Many good things travel through the air, like clouds, the smell of the flowers or the cakes that Grandmother is baking, and the pollen of certain plants that make you sneeze when spring comes. Also, there are many flying animals, from the smallest like the fly, to the largest like the condor. Balloons, helicopters, and airplanes can fly, too. The air also carries things that are not so good, like dust and unpleasant smells from garbage, and very bad things, like some harmful substances called "pollutants," which come from the cities, factories, and agricultural fields. It's very hard to make these pollutants disappear.

Unfortunately, the air is easily dirtied with the smoke
emitted by cars and other motor vehicles and industry
and incinerators, forming gigantic clouds. Have you ever
wondered where the things you own came from? Your toys
and clothes? Many of the products we use were made
in factories. There are thousands and thousands
of factories that emit smoke into the air
from their chimneys.

On a summer's day, Eulalia, who lives
in a mountain village, went on a school trip
to the city. There was a lot of traffic, and they
could hardly see the sun because the sky was gray
from the smoke emitted by the cars, as if there
were a great cloud of fog! When they got off the bus,
the children's eyes started to burn and they began
to cough. And Mar, who has asthma, almost choked!
How can people live well when the air is so dirty?

Out of all the gases in the air, oxygen is one of the most important ones for life because most living creatures need it. When you breathe, the oxygen you take in spreads through your whole body, and that's what enables you to have enough energy to move about and to grow. Your body then converts the oxygen into another gas, called carbon dioxide, which you breathe out.

The greatest source of oxygen on the whole planet is plants. Using sunlight and the chlorophyll that's stored in green leaves, plants carry out a process called photosynthesis, through which they release the oxygen that the rest of the living creatures need. Plants are responsible for the presence of oxygen in the air, which is why it is so important to preserve and take care of the vegetation. At night, the plants also absorb oxygen and release carbon dioxide.

Earth is surrounded by a layer of gas called the atmosphere.
The air in the atmosphere enables people to breathe, and thus
they are able to survive. Otherwise, if we didn't have air, we would
have to wear spacesuits like astronauts do. Can you imagine that?
Furthermore, the atmosphere protects us from dangers
that can come from space, like the sun's rays
and meteorites.

Very high up in the sky, in the upper part of the atmosphere, there is the ozone layer, a band of gas that filters out the sun's rays. If it weren't for the ozone layer, we would get burned! Some years ago, this layer became very thin as a result of pollution. If the ozone layer disappears completely, plant and animal life and also human life will end. We must do something to prevent it from happening!

Sometimes, some of the pollutants that are released by cars
and power plants can fly far away and mix with the water in the
atmosphere to become acidic. When it rains, the raindrops
damage the water in rivers and lakes, contaminate the soil, and
prevent plants and trees from growing; they lose their leaves
and can even die. This rain is called acid rain.

Fortunately, there are many things that can be done to prevent the air from becoming so polluted. Products sold as aerosols, such as deodorants, air fresheners, and insecticides, pollute the air around us very much. You can use others that don't come as aerosols. If you decrease your consumption of unnecessary items, reuse what you can continue to use, and recycle the waste you generate at home, you will also help to keep the air cleaner.

Tell your parents to use the car only when necessary and try to do more things in a single journey. And, if you drive slower, you will emit less polluting gases! You can also pollute less by taking the subway, the train, or the bus when you need to go places. However, if you prefer, you can also walk or go by bicycle. What an excellent invention! And furthermore, it doesn't pollute at all!

Air moves about a lot and it is mischievous and also very
changeable. It can be dry or wet and cold or warm.
When it moves about, it is called wind. Sometimes the wind
is soft and gentle, but some days it seems to be very angry.
It swirls around, forming a gigantic spout that extends from
the ground up to the sky, creating tornadoes. Accompanied
by thunder and lightning, it blows so strongly that it can break,
lift, and carry away whatever gets in its path:
trees, cars, and even people! How scary!

It's windy today! That's great! Now you can go outside and fly your paper kite. When the wind blows, the sky is filled with kites of many colors and very amusing shapes. Thanks to the wind, you can make them fly. You can also dry the clothes you have just washed. Have you ever noticed how the clothes move on the line? If the clothespins don't hold on tightly to the socks, shirts, and trousers, they will fly off!

As you can see, the air is very important. Our planet's climate and the life of the plants, animals, people, and the rest of the living creatures that live on it depend on the air being clean. It is very easy to be careful, and you don't need to make great changes to help to make the air less polluted. I already do, so what about you? It is in your hands. You can do it, too!

Activities

Which one will dry first?

Have you ever wondered why the clothes you hang up never dry all at the same time? You can test it with this experiment. You will need a woolen sweater and another cotton one. Wet them both in water and hang them up to dry outside. Which one do you think will dry first? In a few hours, you will have the answer!

Windmill

Take a 6-inch-long square piece of construction paper. Fold it twice as shown in figure 2, in order to mark the diagonal lines and the middle point. Cut along the four diagonal lines, but without reaching the center (fig. 3). Paste four corners at the center with some glue (fig. 4). Use a pin to make a hole at the point where you have pasted the four corners and fix it to a drinking straw. To make the windmill go round, you should place two pieces of straw at both sides of the windmill. Then place an eraser over the point of the pin so that you don't cut yourself.

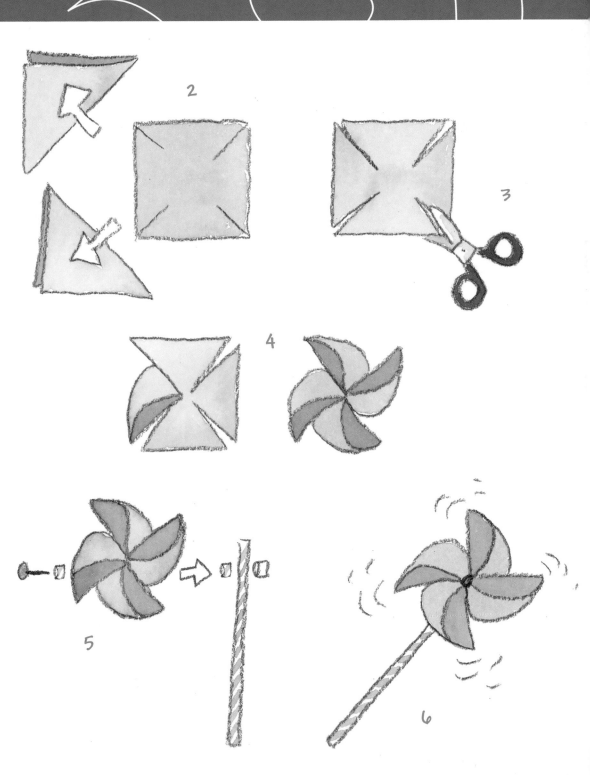

1

2

3

4

Little windmill

Fold three strips of paper in half. Hold the open end of one of the strips and pass it over the closed end of another strip, as shown in figure 3. Do the same with the third strip, so that its fold closes the open part of the second strip. Place the open part of the third strip inside the fold of the first strip (fig. 4). You should make a triangle shape. Gradually pull the ends until the three strips are joined together (fig. 5). Thread a piece of string through the corner and tie a knot in it. If you use different colored paper, it will make a pretty effect. You can assemble several windmills tied to the same piece of string. Tie the other end to a stick. Find an open space, hold the windmill by the stick and run. You'll see how it turns!

5

6

7

You can also place the little windmill by your window, and then you will know when the wind is blowing.

Parents' guide

Respiration (pages 2–3, 10–11)

You can explain to the children in the simplest way how our respiratory system works: The air we take in through our nose or mouth when we breathe in then passes through the pharynx, the larynx, the trachea, and the bronchial tubes until it reaches the alveoli in the lungs, which is where the oxygen in the air enters the blood and is then transported all over the body. Once used, it is released in the form of carbon dioxide, which is expelled from the body. It is important for older children to understand that the objective of respiration is to transport oxygen to the cells that make up the organism and to eliminate the carbon dioxide they release.

Similarly, it is interesting to teach the children that different respiratory systems also exist. For example, many aquatic animals, such as mollusks and fish, breathe through gills. In this case, gaseous exchange (dissolved oxygen and carbon dioxide) takes place directly between the water and the blood via the gills.

Air gets dirty very quickly (pages 6–9, 18–19)

One of the main sources of atmospheric pollution is the combustion conducted by industries, incinerators, and motor vehicles. They release: carbon monoxide, which is much more toxic; carbon dioxide, which intensifies the greenhouse effect; and sulfuric and nitrous oxides that can result in the production of ozone, which, being highly toxic, is very harmful in the troposphere. Furthermore, when they combine with the water in the atmosphere they form the nitric, nitrous, and sulfuric acids that are present in acid rain. This burns the leaves of the plants and can destroy entire forests, lakes, and wetlands.

Other pollutants, however, are released into the air from different sources, such as pesticides and substances that generate unpleasant smells, dust, and so on.

The air in some cities contains so much smoke and dust that when water vapor condenses it forms a kind of fog called smog, from the words "smoke" and "fog."

Photosynthesis (pages 12–13)

Plants contain chlorophyll, the substance that gives them their color. Plants use chlorophyll to capture the energy from sunlight and convert it into chemical energy. This process is called photosynthesis. Plants are living beings and they need to feed themselves, just like animals. Plants absorb water through their roots and, thanks to the energy from sunlight, water is combined with carbon dioxide to produce glucose

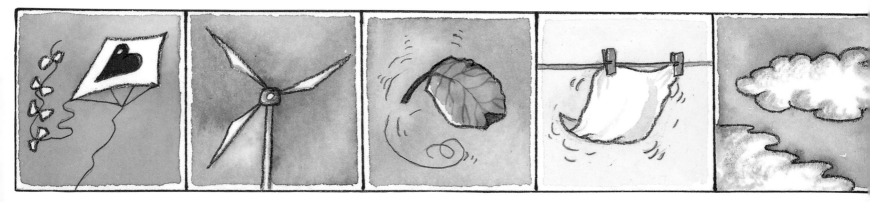

and oxygen. The glucose they produce is used as food and also as energy for growth. Plants release the oxygen they produce through their leaves; oxygen is a very important gas that enables all living creatures to breathe. For this reason, we must preserve and take care of vegetation.

The atmosphere (pages 14–15)
The atmosphere is a layer of gases enveloping the planet. Almost 80 percent of the gas is nitrogen and the great majority of the remainder is oxygen, although other gases are found in small proportions.

The atmosphere extends from Earth's surface to an altitude of about 62 miles. It is divided into different layers: The closest layer to the surface is called the troposphere and extends up to 12 miles. Meteorological events take place in this layer. Higher up, there is the stratosphere, which contains the ozone layer that filters out ultraviolet radiation. Still higher up are the mesosphere, the thermosphere, and the exosphere.

You can explain that the gases present in the atmosphere enable sunlight to reach the surface, but they absorb a large part of the heat emitted by Earth, so that the temperature remains high enough for living creatures.

Some scientists believe that living creatures themselves regulate the composition of the atmosphere and manage to maintain it at a constant level. According to this theory, the planet behaves as a single gigantic organism. If the organism is healthy, the temperature is maintained constant and harmful gases do not accumulate. However, the organism can also become sick; if the composition of the atmosphere changes drastically (for example, if a greater amount of carbon dioxide is released), too much heat is retained and the temperature of the planet increases. This is what we know by the name of climate change. Although the consequences remain unknown, many scientists believe that this could lead to problems: for example, that the polar caps and glaciers would melt, causing the sea level to rise; that it would rain too much in some places and not enough in others; that diseases such as malaria would be transmitted much more easily.

The hole in the ozone layer (pages 16–17)
Until the end of the last century, aerosols contained chemicals called CFCs (chlorofluorocarbons), which are highly unstable and react easily with other substances, such as stratospheric ozone. Hence, for many years, the amount of ozone diminished in a very large area over Antarctica and the affected surface became increasingly large. In 1996, the production of CFCs was prohibited in the Montreal Protocol, and in recent years the "hole" may have begun to close up again. You can explain that it isn't really a hole, but rather a zone in the stratosphere where the ozone is less concentrated.

Cleaner air (pages 20–23)
There are many measures that we can apply to reduce air pollution and it is important for children to learn them. One example would be to limit the use of cars and replace them with public transportation, bicycles, and journeys by foot. Reducing the consumption of manufactured goods can also help. The level of consumption that we have reached encourages excessive production levels by industry. If you only purchase what you need and make children aware of this, you will be doing your bit for this cause.

Blow! air

Original title of the book in Catalan:
Cuidem el Planeta: Bufa! L'Aire
© Copyright Gemser Publications S.L., 2010.
C/ Castell, 38; Teià (08329) Barcelona, Spain (World Rights)
Tel: 93 540 13 53
E-mail: info@mercedesros.com
Website: www.mercedesros.com
Authors: Núria & Empar Jiménez
Illustrator: Rosa Maria Curto

First edition for the United States and Canada published
2010 by Barron's Educational Series, Inc.

All *inquiries should be addressed to:*
Barron's Educational Series, Inc.
250 Wireless Boulevard
Hauppauge, New York 11788
www.barronseduc.com

ISBN-13: 978-0-7641-4545-2
ISBN-10: 0-7641-4545-2

Library of Congress Control No.: 2009943889

Manufactured by: L. Rex Printing Co. LTD.,
Tin Wan, China
Date of Manufacture: August 2010

Printed in China
9 8 7 6 5 4 3 2 1